A Traveller in Uganda

A Historical Article on a Traveller's Experience in Africa

By

William J W Roome

British Library Cataloguing-in-Publication Data
A catalogue record for this book is available from
the British Library

AROUND UGANDA

HAVING a few days of comparative leisure it was a comfort to rest and look back on some of the scenes so hurriedly passed through.

Leaving Mwanza on the lake steamer *Ruzinga* we soon crossed the beautiful Smith Sound, with its rocky cliffs on either side crowned with gigantic blocks of weather-worn granite, which assumed weird shapes, like the playthings of a giant. Probably few of those who have crossed this lake have any accurate idea of its extent. It is rather an inland sea than a lake with its 26,000 square miles of water surface. Under normal conditions it is smooth and calm, with scarcely a ripple on its surface. When a strong wind blows, and gales sweep across the 200 miles from east to west, waves rise rapidly. Even a thousand-ton boat rolls and pitches in a most uncomfortable manner.

After a night at sea early dawn reveals the irregular outline of the mainland, where a small island stands sentinel a few miles off the port of Bukoba. On shore the rocky cliffs reach a higher altitude than in any other spot along the lake-side. Facing the sandy shore, and nestling below the cliff, the marketing town of Bukoba was well laid out by the Germans in pre-war days. Many of the buildings are quaintly erected on the great rock masses scattered over the low-lying land. A jetty runs out into the water for a few hundred yards giving shelter to dhows and small craft, but the lake steamer has to lie out in the roadstead, ready to slip anchor and make for the open at any moment, for with the sweep of a storm from the east over 200 miles of water a tumultuous sea may work up at any time.

When leaving soon after dawn next day, the storm blew

up so rapidly that we had to make straight for the open sea instead of pursuing our course up the coast to the north. For several hours we faced the storm, the boat pitching and rolling almost to the limit of safety. The few passengers on deck soon became cold and hungry. No breakfast was in evidence. At last the steward came up on deck remarking, " We are very sorry, gentlemen, but it is so rough we cannot cook or lay breakfast." It was nearly midday before the storm abated and we could return to our course and secure the long longed-for cup of tea.

Though immense in area the lake is comparatively shallow. It is believed not to exceed more than 300 feet deep in any part. In this respect it is unlike the series of great lakes that traverse the continent from north to south, and which are some of the deepest in the world. Their formation is due to the great split in the earth's crust, which forms the well-known Rift Valley. This lake is merely the shallow basin formed by the ridges of the great rift to the east and the west. Close to the banks are numerous beautiful islands, some of them as much as five miles across. They are usually covered with a dense mass of vegetation. There are also many rocky peaks standing out of the water, with scarcely a blade of grass or a leaf upon them. Such rocks are favourite resting-places for water-birds, especially divers and ducks. Others are the homes of crocodiles and water lizards. The water is beautifully clear and a welcome refreshment to the traveller who has come on board after some long safari across burnt-up lands. Coasting near the shore, where the water is deep enough, the lake-side is an attractive sight as the wavelets flash and ripple in the sunshine, or the bright colours of tropical flowers are visible beneath the shades of trees, while the beautiful water-plants and purple lilies float gracefully in the shallow water. On the rocks and the tree branches diver and other species of larger birds rest with extended wings drying their feathers in the sunshine after their hunting in the water. The brilliant-hued kingfisher and his smaller companions may be seen flitting to and fro.

AROUND UGANDA

Another day brings us from Bukoba to Bukakata, the jumping-off place for the kingdom of Ankole. A few hours' more steaming and we reach Entebbe, the seat of Government clustered around the highest hill, which is crowned by the residence of the Governor of Uganda.

When travelling across the watery waste at certain times of the year, especially towards its close, we appear to see heavy smoke-clouds in the distance, sometimes as much as half a mile in length and several hundred feet in height. They seem to be slowly moving across the surface. These are in reality crowds of tiny may-flies. The pupæ may be noticed as a reddish-brown film covering many hundred square yards on the surface of the lake. From this stage they hatch out. Rising quickly *en masse*, they give the impression of having suddenly appeared from nowhere. Huge clouds of these insects sweep across the lake and envelop the passing steamer that is unfortunate enough to encounter them. It is a most unpleasant experience. To the natives around the lake-shore they come as a welcome variety in diet. They sweep them up in enormous numbers, forming them into cakes, and bake them.

Occasionally when passing inshore, and close to the islands, ghostly figures appear to flit through the grass and brushwood, becoming more visible in the open land. Various forms of buck are seen.

From time immemorial navigation has been carried on around the lake in a particularly interesting form of canoe. This is not the African type of " dug-out.": The shores of the lake do not provide forests with big enough timber for such. The base of the canoe is, however, constructed on the same principle as a " dug-out." On this base the walls are built up of planks sewn together by means of strands from a fibrous creeper, which are passed several times through holes in the adjacent edges bored by a red-hot iron rod. To prevent leaks a fibre pad is applied to the joint on the inner side. This is kept in place by several stems of elephant grass arranged longitudinally. The whole is pressed tightly together by the twine which sews the planks and binds this caulking material at the same time. Another pad of plants and fibre is placed against the joints on the outside. To keep the packing tight it is necessary to tap in slowly and carefully a narrow strip of tough wood under the twine stitches on the outer side. To provide the equivalent of a keel in European boats, the base is prolonged at the fore end into a round projection extending several feet beyond the base of the stem proper. This gives a false prow to the head. It is carved into a notch with several grooves inserted directly beneath. It is usually decorated with a bunch of feathers rising out of a large mop of fluffy raw cotton or grass. From this knob to the prow of the boat itself a cord is hung with long strips of white cotton and a pair of horns or other decoration.

From Entebbe three hours' steaming up the Murchison Gulf and we arrive at the little port of Luzira, the jumping-off place for Kampala, which is connected with the port by a seven-mile railway. The line passes through the papyrus swamps to the higher land at the base of the group of seven hills on which the various sections of the community that make up the capital are situated. The arrival of the weekly train and the steamer marks a busy time for the community. Black, white, and brown will throng the station yard. The road from the station climbs to the hill of Nakasero, known as Kampala, where are the commercial buildings, the various streets of the Indian bazaar, and the European stores. Still rising to the healthier regions, on the crown of the hill are the official residences. From this vantage-point we view the other hills ; Mulago, with its fine hospital, and Makerere, with a modern college, the head-quarters of the Government educational institutions. From this we descend to the valley before the highest hill of all, Namirembe, where the magnificent cathedral of the Anglican Communion crowns the highest point of the country-side, and then pass through the little village of Mengo to the king's residence at the Lukiko and the native Parliament. Following on to the next hill, Rubaga, we have the Roman Catholic cathedral of the White Fathers, and on

4

the opposite hill of Nsambya the buildings of the Mill Hill Roman Catholic Mission.

Kampala has a rapidly-growing community of each of the three national sections, European, Indian, and African. There is an infinite variety of type, from the most elaborately dressed to the most primitive.

The first non-negro from the outer world to penetrate into Uganda was a Baluch named Eisa bin Huissen, who had travelled through Unyamwezi. He eventually arrived at the court of Suna, who was then King of Uganda. He soon won favour, probably owing to his handsome face and large beard, which gave him the name of Muzahya, or the " hairy one." Through him the King of Uganda, his nobles and people, first heard of the world beyond their own country, and it was not long before the Arab traders in Karagwe were invited to his court.

Sheik Snay bin Amir al Harisi was the first to accept. In 1852 this Arab trader stood in the presence of the most powerful king of the best-organised African State then existing, untouched by Arab or European influence. Snay bin Amir remained some time with Suna, and gave him much information about the world outside the Victoria Nyanza, and even beyond the coast of Africa. From him Suna and the Baganda had confirmation of the stories of Isa. They learnt that there really were white men.

The aristocratic clan of the Bahima were much impressed by the story of the white men existing beyond the Nile. They had a tradition that there was a time when they themselves had had a much lighter complexion and blonder hair. They began to wonder whether these white men were their forefathers and might be coming to conquer their country. This Indian returned to the coast and spread news of the wonderful kingdom he had discovered. The result was that the Arab community quickly carried their trade to the interior.

The news came to the ears of the German missionaries Krapf and Rebbmann at Mombasa. Their reports were the indirect cause of Captain Burton's expedition being sent to find out the truth of the story of this comparatively civilised kingdom of Uganda and the great waters around. Thus commenced the close connection between the white and black races of these parts. Burton, however, was unable this time to penetrate into Uganda itself. He became ill and returned to the coast via Unyamwezi, reluctantly acceding to the pleadings of his companion Speke, and allowing the latter with a very poorly equipped expedition to travel with Arabs, or Wanyamwezi, in the direction of the Victoria Nyanza. Thus Speke discovered and named that great lake. His discovery, combined with the information he and his companion had received from the Arabs, convinced him that the main source of the Nile had at last been found.

The history of European intercourse with Uganda thus dates from quite recent times, and has from the first been inextricably bound up with the history of Christian Missions, and more particularly with that of the Church Missionary Society.

In 1843 Krapf, the earliest missionary of the Church Missionary Society on the East Coast of Africa, heard rumours of the existence of a great inland lake in the country of Unyamwezi.

" This rumour was confirmed, and twelve years later, in 1855, two other German Missionaries of the Society, Rebbmann and Erhardt, sent home from Mombasa a remarkable map, known as the ' Slug ' map, showing a vast inland sea, stretching from the Equator to the 13th degree S. Latitude.

" The publication of this map, in 1856, by the Royal Geographical Society, was the first incentive to the discovery, first of the Victoria Nyanza by Speke in 1858, and then of Uganda, by the same traveller, in 1861. His statement, when reporting his great discovery of the course of the Nile, was as strictly true as it was generous : ' The Missionaries are the prime and first promoters of this discovery ' " (Nile source).

If missionaries were thus concerned in the discovery of

EVENING ON LAKE VICTORIA

Uganda they were far more closely connected with its first occupation. In response to an appeal from Sir Henry S. Stanley a party of eight missionaries, under the leadership of Lieut. Shergold Smith, R.N., left for Uganda in 1876, and in June 1877 the first two Europeans to settle in Uganda—Lieut. S. Smith and Rev. T. C. Wilson—arrived at Rubaga, the court of Mutesa, the King of Uganda at that time. Two years later, in 1879, the first Roman Catholic missionaries arrived; in 1890 the Imperial British East Africa Company concluded its treaty with Uganda; and in 1894, seventeen years after the arrival of the first missionaries in Uganda, the British Government proclaimed a Protectorate.

During these early years, in which the Missions stood alone in Uganda, a change to which it would be difficult to find any exact parallel in any other country within so short a time passed over the people.

In 1878 Mr. Wilson was alone in Uganda, his two companions, Smith and O'Neill, having been murdered at the south end of the lake.

At the close of that year he was joined by the great Scottish missionary, Alexander Mackay, and the first Industrial Mission work was begun.

In 1882 the first five converts of the Mission were baptised, and the Native Anglican Church, destined to grow in a short time to very large proportions, came into being.

In 1884 the Rev. James Hannington was consecrated as the first Anglican Bishop of Uganda. The same year Mutesa died and his son Mwanga succeeded.

The Uganda Protectorate contains within its borders four native kingdoms, each complete with its own territory and court. Each is a constitutional monarchy with the "Lukikos," or Houses of Parliament and Ministers of State.

The bulk of the population of each of the native kingdoms consists of the typical Bantu, but in many respects their features and characteristics are more refined. The aristocracy are largely a blend of the true Baganda with the

Hamitic races. Their skins are of a lighter shade, being of chocolate colour rather than black. The Baganda are one of the few tribes of the Bantu race that do not mutilate their persons in any way. They do not knock out, or sharpen, their teeth, nor do they drill their lips, or ears, or practise cicatrisation. They have many characteristics which point them out as a superior type. The eagerness with which they welcome civilisation, and adapt themselves to its progressive tendencies, is a notable characteristic.

The national costume formerly consisted of bark cloth. This has now almost disappeared, except in the outlying districts. They are adopting far too quickly the many vagaries of European dress. The huts that they built formerly were of far better construction than most of the tribes around. These are now disappearing rapidly in favour of the modern wattle and daub house. These again are being supplanted by brick houses of the modern bungalow type.

Every Baganda house of importance has attached to it a series of neatly kept courtyards surrounded by a high fence of reed-work (the universal " ejisakate ").

The Baganda make good pottery, mats, and ropes. Their musical instruments are flutes, harps, horns, and drums. These last are a national institution, the kings' drums and drum-beats all being named individually. Each " saza," or district, sends in drummers to Mengo for a month to beat the kings' drums, taking turns in rotation. They keep the usual domestic animals; their staple food is " matoke " (bananas) and their drink " mwenge " and " mubisi " (fermented and unfermented banana beer).

The Baganda are divided into a number of social or kinship divisions, each of which is an Ejija or clan. The legendary origin of the clan and totem divisions emanated from the decree issued by Kintu, the first King of the Baganda, that certain animals should be taboo to certain families. The real reason for this decree was to prevent the wholesale slaughter of game, as in those days the chief means of livelihood was by hunting. Each family therefore refrained from slaying, or eating, that particular animal which they considered had brought them ill-luck.

The Baganda race has produced an exceedingly large number of capable men. The late Sir Apolo Kagwa was the first African native to be given the K.C.M.G. He was of a striking personality, tall and of massive build. Lacking, perhaps, some of the finer lines of the Bahima, he was strong and intellectual-looking. He first came into prominence about 1886, when King Mwanga tried to destroy the Christian faith and began to massacre the Christians in his Kingdom. Kagwa, then a young man, and another denounced the king. Kagwa's companion was killed, but he escaped. From that time he took a leading part in building up the present-day Uganda.

He was a statesman, administrator, and general, and a great supporter of the Christian faith against the savages of Mwanga, and later the Mohammedan rebels. Besides his military victories and administrative successes, he took a part in every interest of the nation. When the building of a cathedral was embarked upon, and vast quantities of clay were required to be transported some distance, Kagwa inspired the men, women, and children engaged in transporting the clay in baskets, and himself carried load after load on his head.

" He came to England in 1902 as an official representative of Uganda at the Coronation of King Edward, and afterwards wrote an account of his impressions, probably the only faithful record of the Metropolis as seen through the eyes of an African potentate."

The narrative, which was set down in collaboration with his secretary, Ham Mukasa, received a good deal of public notice on account of its quaintness, something of which can be gleaned from such typical quotations as the following :

" Captain Hobart took us away in a fine carriage to the place where we were to stop, which was in a house for strangers, called an ' hotel ' ; the name of our hotel was the Westminster Palace Hotel. When we entered that house it was as if we were going into the house of the King himself; it was magnificent and beautiful beyond praise, and we looked about from side to side admiring it. Though one is praised for restraining oneself and not looking about, it is impossible not to do so in England.

" We went into the room which takes people to the upper floors, and after we had got in the servant shut the door, and told us to sit down, and we sat on the seat; the servant then pulled a small rope and the room took us up. They showed us everything: the dining-room, and the bedroom, and the bath-room, and everything else, and then we sat down, and all the servants, both men and women, came to hear what their work was to be. They know that every visitor has his own habits as to eating and as to drinking tea; one wants to drink every hour, another does not do so; one likes many different kinds of food, another likes a few kinds; they showed us also the things that call the servants to bring the food, or water, and we learned all about them. The work of the servants is this: the men do the cooking, the women make the beds and bring the early tea, and water for washing the face, and clean the boots, and they turn on the bath-water—but we would not let them do this, but did it for ourselves; they also washed our clothes, and lit the fires for us when it was cold—not every day. . . .

" We went to the house of images of all kinds (the British Museum), which contained many wonderful things of long ago, statues of the old kings of all countries and of Egypt. We saw also the body of a man said to be eight thousand years old. We could not understand whether this was true or not, because we see in the Bible that those who calculate the time from the Creation make it out to be nearly six thousand years; and after this one is told that this body is eight thousand years old! Is not this a thing to be wondered at?

" At the Zoo they gave us some biscuits to give to the elephant, which took them out of our hands. We also threw pieces of biscuit into its mouth, and it ate them. It was wonderfully tame and did what it was told, just like a man; they told it to stand on a stone, and it did so; and to put up its trunk, and it did so. We also played with the chimpanzee; its keeper was nursing it like a baby, and he told it to shake hands, and it shook hands like a man. We also saw wonderful

A VILLAGE IN NORTHERN UGANDA

snakes ; two boas from India were as large as the middle of a
crocodile, and each eats a goat every day. I also saw a turtle
as large as a pig, and a giraffe that was much taller than an
elephant ; perhaps it was as much as 20 or 22 ft. high, and it
was still young. A great many people come in to see these
animals, perhaps as many as a hundred thousand every day ;
I do not quite know, as one meets numbers of men, women,
and children wherever one goes. Do not think they can just
walk in—not so at all ; they first have to pay something, and
they can then go in and see the animals.

" We saw the lights of Southampton, which were like stars
or comets. These lights can be seen five miles away. When
one hears the ships trumpeting anyone who knows how cows
bellow that have been raided in war would understand when
I say they bellowed like that, though I only compare them to
cows on account of the numbers—the noise they make is far
greater, greater even than the trumpeting of an elephant :
they go on all night, coming in and going out, and never leave
off their noise ; the ships trumpet as they come in and trumpet
as they go out, and you hear a great noise all the time with
the large ships and the small ships, and the moaning of the
sea and the noise made by the screws of the ships as they
go by. . . ."

The following account of some of the clans of the Baganda
has been given by the Rev. T. B. Fletcher after thirty years
amongst the people :

" Most of the Clans in Buganda claim to have come to
Buganda with Kintu, the founder of the present ruling house.
This is in a way natural. Yet one or two of these clans claim
to have been here when that man came into the country.
The Lung Fish (mamba) claim this ; saying that they were
the ruling power in the country at that period and one branch
of the clan go so far as to say that Kintu was of that clan and
that after he was firmly established, he seceded from them.
The branch of the clan, who recognise Gabunga as their head,
make that claim, whereas the branch that recognise Nankere
as their head, say that they came with Kintu. There seems
to have been a division in the clan during the reign of the
Kabaka Tembo, the sixth ruler of the present ruling house.

6

13

The clan that can give many generations of men and their doings in the land previous to the establishment of the present dynasty is not to be easily set upon one side, and their claims must be recognised. Bukandebukakoma was the founder of the clan, and he is supposed to have settled at Mbale in Mawokota, very near to where the Kampala-Masaka road crosses the Entebbe-Toro road. From that place the followers of the clan took possession of practically all the land lying to the east of the Kampala-Masaka road, with centres at Kiumu, Jungo, and Kasanji, all close to Entebbe and Budo.

" The cause or reason given for the settlement upon this side of the Lake Victoria is that Mubiru, one of their leaders, was in Bumogera, and after committing an offence was heavily fined. This fine he was unable to pay, so he and his following took to canoe and came round the lake. Their first port of call in Buganda being Busagazi in Kyagwe, then on to Ngogwe and Ziba, and finally settled at Kiumu, Bweya, near Entebbe. The fable of the battle between the tortoise and the snake took place before the arrival of Kintu, according to many of the best authorities. This fable was most probably founded upon a battle between Nfudu (tortoise) and Bemba, who were of the same clan. Many of the customs followed by the present ruling house date from that period, such as the going to Budo by the Kabaka upon his accession to the kingdom to be instructed by the chief Semanobe in the use of the spear and the shield.

" With the exception of one or two clans, the leaders of which came into the country at a later date, it appears that all the leaders in the country at this early period were of one stock and that every man's hand was against his fellow. Whether the Lung Fish clan were in possession with one or two other clans will never be settled. From the very earliest times the Lung Fish clan was most powerful and the strongest in the country.

" The tradition runs that when Kintu was firmly established as the head of the nation he called the leading landowners (butaka) to Njagalabwami, Magonga, in the country of Busuju ; to settle the question of the clans. All said that they were of one clan. The plan adopted by the ruler was to make a feast and if any of the food eaten made the partaker ill, that was to be his totem. This may have been the case ; yet it does not account for the many totems that are not edible. I am of the opinion that Kintu, to whom all give the credit of the introduction of the clan system into this country, seeing the kind of mob with which he had to deal, introduced the system for the safety of life and property, a system of freemasonry.

" The head of the Lung Fish (mamba) is Gabunga, with Makamba, as, so to speak, chief justice of the clan. Yet the second division of the clan, with a small fish as the totem (maguya), has Nankere for the head. Many have been the discussions as to the real head, and this question will never be settled. The head of the clan, Gabunga, is treated more like a prince of the royal blood than as an ordinary Muganda. He is buried in the same way as the ruling monarch. From time immemorial Gabunga has been the head of all the canoes upon the Buganda side of the Lake Victoria, also lord of the Sese Islands. As Admiral of the Fleet he is responsible, not only for the making of the canoes, but their upkeep and supply of paddlers.

" Considering that practically all the intercourse with the outer world which the Baganda possessed for generations was by means of the Lake Victoria, the country west of Toro being unknown, and the country not opened up, this individual was a person of might and influence.

" Most of the 'butaka' or lands belonging to the clans, which means that members of some importance lie buried there, are in the country around the shores of the Lake Victoria. Only five out of some seventy-seven of these are in the country inland.

" During the period of time from Kintu to the present ruler there have been some thirty-eight on the throne. Of these seven have been of this Lung Fish clan, that is to say, sons of the Lung Fish clan, the custom being that the Kabaka follows the clan of his mother. This is only applicable to him and not to other Baganda. During the same period ten members of this clan have had the position of first minister (katikiro), five have held the office of Kimbugwe. This office was practically the second in the State until it was done away with a few years ago.

" The members of this clan follow a custom that is not allowable in any other clan in Buganda, intermarriage in the clan, for marriage with a person of another branch of the clan is permitted. The clan being so numerous may be the reason for this custom.

"As in the other clans, this one has names for men and women of the clan. These names until of late years were not given to members of other clans. The leading names for the male section of the clan are—Mubiru, Nsubuga, Bwete, Kizito, Sempagama, Galiwango, Kasozi, Bunjo, Ndiwalana, and Luwandaga. For the female section—Namubiru, Nansubuga, Namutebi, Nakatereke, Namugaba, and Nasuna.

"The clan has three distinct drum-beats, which every member of the clan knows.

"The clan of Colobus Monkey (Ngeye) claims to be one of the oldest in the country. It certainly had a separate existence very early in the annals of the country. From this clan Kintu obtained his wife, to whom is attached the fable as to how death entered into the country, by her disobedience to her husband's orders. This woman was the mother of three sons and one daughter, the sons were Wunya Kiwewa, Malanga, Chwa Nabaka ; the daughter, Nasolo. Wunya was given part of Bunyoro as his portion, Malanga was lost at the same time as his father Kintu at Magonga, Chwa Nabaka succeeded his father as ruler of Buganda. As to the question of Kintu and his son being lost, i.e. one day they went out and were never seen again, the reason being that they fell into one of the deep pits (nyanga) that exist about the neighbourhood of Magonga. Members of this clan have been few who have risen to offices of the first rank in the country, only one to be the Kabaka, one to fill the office of Katikiro, and three the office of Kimbugwe. They do not appear to have been of a pushing disposition, for out of the many hundreds of women who were wives of the various kings, only some thirty-one were women of this clan. Yet this clan had definite work for the king allotted to them. For several generations of the kings a member was the head of the king's serfs or slaves (Sabadu). At the present time the man in charge of the prisoners and chief executioner is of the clan, and he also holds the office of chief undertaker to His Highness. Kauka, another member, is head goat-herd. Wabulakayole, also a member, is the head thatcher to the king and the leading chiefs. Kisawe is the goldsmith of the palace, making the brass bracelets worn by the household. Although the members of the clan are called the grandparents of the king, they were made hewers of timber and drawers of water for the royal household, for, in addition to the above, the drinking water of the king is brought by the members of this clan, and they are known by the name of Balindalu'zi (keepers of the well).

" They only possess one drum-beat, ' Kintamye.' Their plots of butaka are fairly well scattered all over the country, numbering some fifty-three plots."

THROUGH UGANDA TO KAVIRONDO

NAMIREMBE CATHEDRAL, crowning the heights of the greatest hill around Kampala, was the last of the capital to be visible, many miles away, as I set out for another safari to the coastal regions. This time I was to travel as far as possible by cycle. It was the cotton season, and I passed quite a number of *hamali* (Swahili for man-hauled) carts—a very primitive, cumbersome, and slow means of progress. Towards evening as we were cycling along the country road we found several of these preparing for the night camping by the roadside. One of them was surrounded by a picturesque group, ground sheets were spread under the cart for their beds, cooking was going on round the camp-fire, and the men squatted around a " reader." The group was at evening prayer by the roadside, for many of these " hamali " men are Christians, and they carry the only literature they need with them.

After a cycle journey of fifty-five miles from Kampala we reached the blue waters of the Napoleon Gulf of Lake Victoria. The glistening waters light up the panorama as one comes over the crest of the last hill, some seven miles from the lake-side. Beyond the waters stretch the range of blue hills where Bishop Hannington ended his great inland journey, and met his martyrdom.

The waters of the Napoleon Gulf, which have been described as the Source of the Nile, narrow in an estuary which passes over the Ripon Falls. This is the outlet from the lake. An easy run downhill and we are alongside the ferry, and old Father Nile. What pictures, what thoughts, what memories pass through my mind as I watch these fast-flowing waters pouring with their ceaseless thunder over the great rocky barrier ! To have seen the mighty river for the greater part of its 4,000 miles, from its source in the far-away Ruanda hills to its mouth in the Mediterranean, is to taste to the full its romance and fascination.

The town of Jinga stretches along the opposite bank. *Jinga* stands for " rocks," and a rocky spot it is—rock seemingly almost red-hot some days as one climbs the bank and sets out for the dusty town. Jinga is a great port. During the cotton season it is the busiest on the lake-side. From the pier and its bustling crowd the road bends round over the hill, and we are quickly passing along its one crowded street.

A favourite walk for travellers by the lake steamer during its day's wait at this point is for some half a mile round the bend to the Falls along a sun-baked cliff. Below, the waters gleam smooth and almost motionless. Beyond the bend, where the estuary narrows, crowds of jagged rocks stand out above the water. Bare and threatening they look as the water circling around begins to eddy. The roar of the falling waters comes to the ears before they are visible. The calm smoothness of their surface has given place to a wild hurrying and scurrying over the masses of broken rock before taking the great plunge.

The Falls are three in number, divided by masses of rock scarcely visible under the dense foliage. After the last rush and tumble they go raging and foaming far round the next bend. The nearest fall from the Jinga side is the narrowest of the three. The centre of the raging mass is dark, deep, and gloomy owing to the depth of water over the brim. On either side the seething mass has broken into foam on the rocky barriers. Of the three falls the finest is that on the Uganda side, seldom visited because of the difficulty of access. As we watch the white mass of foam a dark object shoots upward straight at the face of the falling water, to disappear as quickly as it came. One after another the fish attempt the impossible. Twenty and thirty pounders jump right out of the water in their vain endeavour. Large birds of several species glide to and fro over the foaming waters in search of smaller fry. Then they perch on a branch or rock above the turmoil with their out-stretched wings drying in the sun.

Along the river numbers of rocky islands add to the beauty of the scene. A ripple on the smoother waters may indicate the movement of hippo or crocodile. The Nile, with unused energy, races through the rocky cliffs for some three miles until another jagged break across the river gives birth to the Owen Falls. These are not so high, but are even more majestic in their continuity as the water passes over the rocky barrier from bank to bank.

Thus the scene by day. I have camped several times alongside the rushing stream in the deep velvet darkness of the night, and under the mystic light of the moon. Then the waters have a magic that will never be forgotten.

From Jinga, a twenty-eight mile cycle run and we are at the outskirts of Iganga, the next centre of civilisation, for the night. Early next morning we are on the road again, making for Nabumali at the foot of Mount Elgon. After a long day's cycle run under a specially broiling sun, we came towards evening to the swamp of Mpologoma. Resting for a while in the afternoon at the hamlet of Nabitendi I received a warm welcome from the local chief. As an old pupil of King's School, Budo, the High School of Uganda, he was a well-educated and capable man, speaking English fluently. He took me round his estate and showed me the well-worn local church, and pointed out the site he had given for a new one. He kindly sent on a messenger to the ferry, and another as our guide and assistant for the difficult crossing.

The Mpologoma is an arm of Lake Kioga, and is a swamp about a mile wide overgrown with papyrus. As we passed along the narrow open waterway we were surrounded by papyrus-grass, flower, and fern, which were beautiful both in mass and detail, but they shut out every breeze till the atmosphere was like an oven. Bird and insect life were most prolific and interesting, though in the circumstances one would have been glad to have been spared the latter.

Here the dreaded tsetse fly, of sleeping-sickness fame, has its habitat, with a few of its less harmful comrades. It was now getting dusk, and we were glad to find a cluster of huts that constituted the rest-camp.

As we resumed our journey early next morning the giant mass of Elgon loomed on the far horizon above the mists. After a very hot morning's run we were glad to rest in the cool shade of the " gombola " or courthouse at Butalega. As we rested within its mud walls the local chief came and gave us a friendly welcome. He was followed by a lad with a teapot and cups on a tray, for our kind host was doing his best to entertain me in a becoming manner.

After midday we resumed our cycling up hill and down dale, over the foothills of the mighty mountain near which the Mission station of Nabumali is situated. We had now passed through the country of Busoga. This originally consisted of a number of tribes all more or less in a state of war with each other. At one time the country was so thickly populated by people rich in food and cattle that Bukedi, one of the southern counties, was regarded as the " Promised Land " by caravans coming from the coast, after their three months' travel, so often over waste lands. Sleepy sickness, however, spread rapidly through the southern districts bordering on the lake. The destruction thus commenced was intensified by a terrible outbreak of smallpox in 1900, and further devastation came in 1908, the time of the big famine. The greater part of Bukedi, " the land of the naked " is now bush, inhabited by pigs, leopards, and hyenas.

Three of the tribes of the Bukedi district belong to the Bantu group—the Bagishu, Banyuli, and Bagweri. Tradition says that this district was inhabited by Nilotic negroes till some hundreds of years ago when the Baganda commenced the invasion of the country and mingling with the neighbouring tribes became relatives of the Busoda tribes.

In the great papyrus swamps there is a curious race called the Bakeni. They build their huts and live on the floating islands of papyrus. They move about in small dug-out canoes, and eke out a precarious existence by fishing and ferrying travellers. Owing to the inaccessibility of their dwellings they are very independent and live in dread of the dwellers on the dry land.

Arrived at Nabumali I was very kindly received by the Rev. and Mrs. Banks. The station is beautifully located on rising ground at the foot of Mount Kokonjero, or " White Chicken Mountain," the precipitous mass extending for about seven miles in length and rising 3,500 feet above the plain. It is connected with Mount Elgon by a long ridge. Mount Elgon itself, 14,140 feet above sea-level, is credited with being one of the greatest of extinct volcanoes. As one gazes up at its mighty mass and sees the clear-cut outline of the great lip, and realises at the same time that this is some ten miles across, one tries to conjure up some idea of the eruption that caused it. Deep forests clothe the lower slopes up to the rocky battlements of the crater walls.

The lands of the foothills are very fertile, and there is a dense population. The principal race is the Bagisu, of which there are three sub-tribes with varying language dialects. This Mount Elgon country is believed to possess some of the most archaic forms of Bantu speech. The Bagisu live as high up as an altitude of 9,000 feet where the cold at times is intense. Amongst these hill-clans there are some of a particularly primitive type, short, wiry men with long arms, small heads, and bearded faces. Their national dress is a goatskin for adult men, while the ladies favour a short skirt of banana leaves. Among the hill-clans the men usually adorn themselves with heavy iron collars and iron arm-rings. From their ears they suspend rings, shells, etc. The women wear anklets, bracelets, and bead neck-laces. As a race they are industrious. Men and women work alongside each other in the fields. A wife is usually priced according to her capacity for work. There are numerous other tribes to the north of the mountain, in the far wilderness towards the Sudan and Abyssinia. One of these is the Banuli, who represent a transition between the Basoga and the Bagisu. Bark cloth is their national costume. Another tribe, the Baguri, was one of the first in this district to come under European influence. The Balegeniji are an interesting race of one of the high mountain ridges. Many of them are tri-lingual, speaking Lugishu, Nandi, and old Lugweri. Within the mountain area there are also the Bakidea, Baligenyi, and Basabea. To the north, in the more open country, are the Ngabaro, Ngeroni, Karamoja, Bakora, Turkana, Turkwell, Tapuza, and Dabossa.

It is held by some (and there is a native tradition to support the theory) that Mount Elgon is the original home of the Baganda and Basoga. If that is so, one would expect to find between the Elgon aborigines and the Basoga a tribe which had some of the characteristics of both. The Banyuli supply this link. Their own tradition is to the effect that they came from the Kavirondo country, or Lake Victoria, to Banyuli in Busoga, from whence half of them penetrated north of the Mpologoma to their present home in the Bukedi district. This migration was probably in the nature of a return towards their place of origin, under pressure from the Nilotic Kavirondo.

A day's run over mountain roads brought us to the frontier of Kenya Colony. After wading across the Lewkaka River, which forms the boundary, we reached more level country. The first night was spent at Malakisi, some fifteen miles within the new territory, and we began to miss the hospitality of the Baganda and tribes through whom the journey so far had been made. They had been ever ready to bring the essentials for a night's camp-fire—wood, water, bananas for the boys, and the inevitable diminutive chicken for the " Masungu " or white man. But we soon discovered the same was not to be expected on this side, and camping between Mission stations became more difficult. At sunset Elgon showed up its golden head and the foot-hills, now left behind, were clothed in purple—a magnificent colour picture, with its russet-tinted foreground of rocks and grasses.

A heavy day's journey of fifty miles, over roads no self-respecting cyclist at home would think of taking his machine long, ended at Butere. On the way, near the old town of Mumias, Hannington's old track was once again crossed. This was one of his last stopping places. From Mumias to Butere a fine new road of ten miles was being brought into cycling condition.

Butere is the centre of the C.M.S. work in the Bantu section of the great Kavirondo people. The tribe with its subdivisions numbers over a million, about equally divided between Nilotics and Bantu. These Kavirondo are amongst the most primitive of the tribes, and were long left unreached ; now they are proving some of the most promising of people in this part of the Colony.

It was a pleasure to meet Chief Yusufu Malama again at his new home situated on a hill-top about two miles from the Mission, with a magnificent view over the whole plain to Mount Elgon. He is a middle-aged man of intelligent features, and with a kindly countenance.

From Butere I went on to East Kitosh on foot. This station is situated on a spur of Mount Elgon, forty-one miles distant, and I had hoped to reach it in two days ; but the great rains, heavy floods, and a guide who did not know the way, lengthened the march to sixty miles. It would have been impossible to cycle through the district, which was suffering from an unprecedented rainfall. Every river and stream was in flood.

On approaching the Nzoia River at Mumias, ten miles north of Butere, I found the strong steel bridge had just been washed away, and left no means of crossing. For some time it looked as if there would be considerable delay in reaching the other side of the flood. After a while we found there was a " dug-out " some couple of miles down the river, although we could not obtain information as to the possibility of crossing by it. We started in this direction and at last discovered the ancient ship drawn up on the reedy bank, and a few people lying down watching the rushing torrent. After examining the vessel, which was certainly very rotten in its upper works, and finding a crew willing for a consideration to try the venture, we decided

A MOUNTED KAVIRONDO CHIEF, KENYA

to make the attempt. Dividing our forces so as to lighten the cargo I got in with the first party. We crouched down as low as possible to steady the canoe. A few swift pulls of the paddle and we were out in the raging torrent, in a race for life. We were soon carried downstream for a couple of hundred yards and gradually drifted into the reeds of the opposite bank. Alas, there was no bank, but a vast reedy swamp about two to three feet deep through which we had to wade. Glad we were, however, to be safely over.

A few miles and we found some grass huts and commenced preparations for a night's encampment. The rain had just ceased, and the whole party were soaking. There was one hut with a roof that kept out most of the storm, though its walls consisted of bare poles. However, it sheltered us. My porters were Butere men. Soon after getting into camp, and while some were preparing a fire, others withdrew to the lee side of the hut to secure some shelter. The centre of the group produced a bundle of apparently old banana leaf from his loin-cloth. This he began to carefully unfold. After a number of wrappings of leaf there was a small piece of calico. Inside was a copy of the Gospel of St. Luke. This he had purchased just before leaving Butere, and at the first opportunity he was keen to read it aloud ! Long before thinking of drying their clothes, or of obtaining food, they gathered round this treasure. Later on, when the storm had quite ceased, the reading continued around the camp-fire. Whenever we rested during these days on the roadside, or in camp, this book appeared.

We had a cold, damp night, and at dawn were glad for the march. Mount Elgon was a striking picture away to the north. We had eighteen miles to cover to our nearest camping ground at Mabiro. The track was fairly good and the scene enlivened with villages in every direction and many herds of cattle. We hoped to have reached camp early, but after fifteen miles or so we came to a sudden halt in the valley. A stream that should have been easily crossed was another raging torrent. My men sat down on

17

26

the bank and looked at the waters. There were about twenty others on the opposite bank doing the same. There was not even an old " dug-out " here. For some time nobody on either side would venture into the water. Investigations up and down river for a considerable distance gave nothing more promising in the way of a ford. After various attempts I put a man on each side of me, and induced another couple of men on the other side to see if we could meet in the middle. The water proved to be not more than waist deep. The greatest trouble was the rush of the torrent over a rough, rocky bed. With the help of these men I was soon safely on the far bank. It was now my turn to sit down and smile. With great palaver the respective parties crossed to the opposite banks. After a delay of about an hour and a half every one had safely changed sides. After a few more miles' march, dry clothes and a warm drink were very acceptable.

From Mabiro to East Kitosh should have been only a twenty-mile march. When we set off soon after dawn there was a cloudless sky. The bold outline of Elgon showed up sharply on the horizon. By noon I expected to be safely at Kitosh. Before noon I knew we had covered the twenty miles, but there was no sign of the Mission station. I noticed my guide was very uncertain as to the way. At last he confessed that he did not know where the Mission was. We were now in a district with few people, and no one to inquire from. My guide decided the best thing he could do was to sit down. This he would have been quite content to do indefinitely. However, away to the east I saw a little cloud arising, not bigger than a man's hand, and understood the portent. At this time of the year the mornings are brilliant and cloudless. About noon the first signs of a coming storm appear in the east. In an hour's time the whole sky may be overcast. Within another hour the regular afternoon storm would have burst. We had experienced this day after day. It seemed unlikely that we should find shelter before the storm reached us. I decided to be my own guide, and climbed a hill to scan the far horizon in every direction. In the distance were numbers of villages, but nothing to distinguish one from another. At last, miles away, I saw what looked like a couple of hayricks which were decidedly bigger than the indigenous hut.

Seeing no road or track in that direction, I set off in hope across country. Most of the porters had lagged behind. It seemed wiser to try and make for shelter than wait for a laggard lad with a lunch-box. For nearly a couple of hours we struggled on across country till we met the wind blast that we knew was the precursor of the afternoon thunder-storm. I was apparently within a mile of the " hay-stacks," but just as the storm burst in all its fury a deep valley impeded progress. It was a struggle to get through facing the welter of the storm. Climbing the last hill, I found a track leading to the house. At the porch there seemed no evidence of human friendship. Exhausted, soaked, and chilled to the bone, I fell down on a bundle of grass and was thankful at last to be under the shelter of a verandah. Finding no response from indoors, I looked round for some indication of native life. At last a youngster slyly peeped round a corner. After a while he ventured near the stranger. I could find out no information from him, so gave him my card with an indication to take it to the white man, wherever he might be. Another ten minutes had passed and still no other sign of humanity. I decided I had better be my own guide again. Following another track than that by which I had arrived I heard singing, and realised that the school must be in session. I followed the song to the second " hay-stack," and noticed the portal of the school. It was crowded with young folks, and their teacher was on the platform at the far end. I must have looked a quaint figure going up the aisle. As perfect strangers to each other we indulged in the usual greeting. Directly I indicated that I represented the Bible Society, he immediately exclaimed, " Oh, we are so glad to see you ! Will you address the school ? "

I had left a watery track along the mud beaten floor of

the aisle, and by this time was standing in a pool of water on the platform. I could hardly speak for cold and exhaustion, so I merely replied that, glad as I would be to address the school, I would like to do so on a little later occasion. I am afraid this incident led to the early closing of the school. My new-found friend Mr. Ford returned with me to his home and discovered Mrs. Ford. It was not long before I was thawing beside a glowing fire. Though the line of the equator passes close to these regions, at this altitude of some 6,000 feet one can shiver on the equator after such a storm.

It was indeed a joy to have a week-end rest with these Americans, and we found a common association in another Mission in which we were both interested. The station lies close under the mighty mass of Mount Elgon, and I was anxious to make its further acquaintance. On the Monday Mr. Ford kindly arranged a safari for me to Chief Marangu, and on beyond to Kibingeyi. I enjoyed a night's hospitality at the home of this well-known chief. Next morning we set off with one of his guides for the homes of the Troglodytes, some way up the mountain-side. After a couple of hours' march we found ourselves on the summit of one of the foothills with a wide-spreading panorama around, and a rocky cliff-face rising hundreds of feet behind. Over this descended one of the many mountain streams. The fall would be about a hundred feet. From our point of vantage there was a little track that led in between the rocks close behind the spray of the fall. The last twenty yards was a difficult climb, with the spray falling over the slippery path. At the top of this we found ourselves in a mighty cave. The entrance to the cave must have been about twenty feet wide, and nearly as high. Inside the area opened out into many darkened recesses. There was an accumulation of rubbish, and the wooden erections were indications of the old cave dwellings. These recesses passed right into the darkness. How far we did not find out. Not only the folks themselves but the oxen found refuge here from their enemies, the cattle raiders of the Masai. There appeared to be three separate entrances to the cave. At each were the remains of a strong stockade. While we were there several folks came in and visited the caves, looking for rock salt, which is to be found in the inner recesses. Some of these caves are still occupied, but most of the Troglodytes have been compelled to live in the valley. While in their old haunts the local authorities found it difficult to compel the payment of " hut " tax. When the ubiquitous tax-collector appeared they retired to the innermost darkened recesses. They were never " at home " when he called. Probably they were conscientious objectors, and claimed that their caves were not " huts." The order went forth that they must build huts in the open country below. These Troglodytes must leave their granite mansions for mere mud and grass hovels.

Back at Kitosh, arrangements were made for a march southward to Kisumu, the port on Lake Victoria and terminus of the Uganda Railway.

The Nzoia River passes within seven miles of the Mission. The bridge over it had been washed away in the recent storms. Some of the Mission porters had been sitting, with their loads, for four days on the other side of the river, unable to get across. Mr. Ford kindly came down with me to assist in the transit. With the aid of a dug-out, and with careful navigation, we arrived at the far side. I resumed the march for some twenty miles to Malava. On the way there was one more river to cross. There should have been a good bridge. This had followed the example of others, and had disappeared in the flood. There was a group of natives squatting on the far side, and they mourn-fully informed our party that the river could not be crossed, it was too deep. After a long search upstream we found a " crow's nest." The trees on either bank spread out their branches till they almost met. Climbing these we were able to spread some sticks across, and tie them sufficiently securely to make a temporary bridge. If we could not swim like fish we could at least climb like monkeys. It was a beautiful country, with Mount Elgon to the north and the long blue range of the Nandi escarpment about a dozen miles to the east.

When about five miles from my destination I was met by Mr. Chilson and his motor-cycle, on the back wheel of which I finished my journey, and enjoyed this family's hospitality. He had recently opened this pioneer station on the edge of the forest region. Next day he took me the first dozen miles on his motor-cycle, till the road became too bad for this helpful means of progress. I then continued the march for another ten miles to the Lirhanda Mission.

The next day's march was a short one of ten miles to Kaimosi, where a large farm had been established and saw-mill and one of the largest hospitals in these parts.

The following morning I went on to Aldai, the first station, in this direction, of the Africa Inland Mission. It was an eighteen-mile march over mountain and valley, extremely picturesque but very heavy going. Crossing the heights one obtained wonderful panoramic views. Along the valleys we were shut in narrow forest tracks, some along flowing streams. My porters had difficulty in getting through the forest. We were considerably delayed and again caught in the violent afternoon thunder-storm. In a few moments the path became a brook. The last few miles were through a wild storm in a ragged country. At last we caught sight of a " tin " roof in the distance, and I knew we were at our journey's end.

We were now in the land of the Nandi people, notorious as great lion and leopard hunters. I have witnessed the gathering of the clans for one of these hunts, but, as I had to hurry on, could not wait to see the result in the capture of a brace of leopards. The following story was given to me by an eyewitness.

When a lion is spotted the village drum is beaten and the clans gather from every direction. Calls are shouted from hill to hill, giving the direction the lion is taking. Immediately, men gather from all quarters, armed with spears and shields. They advance in a huge circle and, gradually closing in, they tighten their ranks till the king of the forest is entrapped in an armed circle of a few hundred yards. Still closing in, the hunters form several ranks deep. Seeing that he is surrounded the lion either charges or crawls under a bush, as he did on this occasion. Then two men went in to cut down the bush. The lion sprang at the first, who caught hold of its beard and rammed his left arm into the open mouth. The other man sprang on its back, pulled its ears, and held it tight till the warriors came up and bathed their spears in its blood. This is real sport and requires far more courage than the long shot of the white man's modern rifle. When Roosevelt travelled through East Africa he went to this Nandi tribe to see what lion-hunting really was like.

The Nandi tribe are particularly interesting, as they indulge in a species of sun-worship. The god of the Nandi is the sun which they call Asista, or, without the article, Asis. In physical type, language, and customs, they closely resemble the Masai. Careful investigators have suggested the possibility of the relation of these people to the Semites of old. There are said to be indications of Canaanitish origin. One indication of this is the word for " Devil." These investigators, Hollis and others, believe this Chemos had been originally the same as the sun-god of the ancient Moabites.

Both the Nandi and the Masai married women wear ear-rings of a similar design. They are discs of closely coiled and polished wire. With the Nandi these discs are as much as six inches in diameter. With the Masai they are smaller. In both cases the discs are attached to the ear lobes, which in the case of the Nandi hang so far down as to rest one on each breast. In addition the Masai married women wear wide necklaces or collars made of polished wire, which rest on the shoulders and the upper part of the chest. The Nandi sun-worship gives these some possible original symbolic meaning, the sense of which is no doubt obscure to the wearers to-day. The Masai word for serpent is *Asuria*, and that for the brass discs worn as ear ornaments *Surutya*. This word is supposed to be associated with

Suriha, the sun-god mentioned in Syrian inscriptions. This again with the Hebrew word *Seraph*, meaning "burning one."

Aldai is within sixteen miles of the railway station of Kibigori on the Uganda Railway. There were only three trains a week, so I had to leave next morning in time to catch the 7.50 a.m. At 3 a.m. we set off by lantern light. The Mission station is situated on a plateau 6,500 feet above sea-level. There is a precipitous descent of 2,000 feet to the plain below, where the railway runs. As we set off the darkness was intense. Even with the aid of a lantern we had rough going. Fortunately, just as the worst part of the track was reached that involved sliding over rocks, and wading through streams down the mountain-side, the sun began to rise over the distant mountains on the other side of the plain. It was a magnificent sight, and alone worth the effort of getting up so early. The first rays of sun lit up the cloud-enveloped valley. The rose-tinted peaks would have been a delight to any artist. The deep ravine down which the path led and the towering cliffs on either side of the path, only half lit with the dawn's rays, all combined to make one of Nature's happy panoramas. The sun's heat soon dried up the mists. We could see the thread of the railway cutting across the plain.

Reaching the lowest level we had a mile of wading through black cotton-soil swamp, a grand finale to the morning's march, and arrived at Kibigori station with a quarter of an hour to spare. The twenty-five miles to Kisumu were covered in an hour and a half, and I revelled in the luxury of a railway carriage.

During this march of 275 miles I had passed through ten language areas and visited the Mission stations of five societies, discussing the problems of publications and translations of the Scriptures.

Kisumu is the sun-baked administrative centre, lake port, and railway terminus of these regions, beautiful for situation on a rocky elevation surrounded by precipitous mountains. So largely sheltered by the surrounding hills, it possesses a monotonous record of high temperature. The Government and European residential quarters are to some extent shaded by avenues of acacia trees. There is no hotel for weary travellers, but a "dak" bungalow provides a shake-down and hospitality at the end of the railway and commencement of the lake journey.

The Kavirondo race, with its various tribal units, was up to recent years amongst the most primitive of mankind. A few years ago an American who had travelled the world said that the strangest sight he had seen anywhere was Adam and Eve boarding the train at Kisumu! Now in nearly every district some form of clothing is worn.

The greater part of their land is rich and fertile. Huts crowd in every direction, the density of some localities being three hundred per square mile. Every rising hill has its hamlet, surrounded by patches of cultivation, peas, beans, maize, sweet potatoes, and bananas. Many of the country roads are lined with avenues of russets and greens of the nsambia tree or wattle.

From Kisumu I had another circular tour to make. In the first march of eighteen miles we climbed the escarpment for 2,000 feet to Maseno, where the extensive Mission buildings, educational, industrial, and medical, range along the crest of the hill, looking down 2,000 feet to the Kavirondo Gulf of Lake Victoria and across the plain to the far-distant hills.

The Kavirondo people can be placed in two distinct races, the Nilotic, and the Bantu. The former constitute the bulk of the population to the north-west and also skirting the eastern shores of Lake Victoria as far south as Tanganyika. They have a close family relationship with the Shilluks of the Nile valley. In the course of the last two or three centuries they have gradually migrated south to more fertile lands. At the Great Lakes the migration divided. Some clans of the tribes went west to Lake Albert and into territory that is at present part of the Belgian Congo. The language of the Nilotic is for all practical purposes uniform throughout the area. "Luo," as it is known, has few variations. By way of contrast, the Bantu tribal units are split up into about a dozen sections, each with its own distinctive dialect, such as Bagisu, Deko, Hanga, Isuka, Nyore, Myala, Ragoli, Sotso, Suka, Tachoni, Tako, Tireki. Of these the Hanga is again subdivided into Kisa, Kihyo, Maragi, and Samia. This division naturally complicates the language problem immensely, with the inevitable result that Swahili as a *lingua franca* is largely doing duty as the common speech of the people in administration and social services.

The next station is within four miles and is situated on the hill-top at Bunyore. Ten miles farther on Maragoli is situated on another hill-top surrounded with a forest of wattle. From the rocky hill-top of Maragoli there is a magnificent panorama of the greater part of the area of the Kavirondo country. Sixty miles to the north, Mount Elgon bounds the landscape, while forty miles to the south another mountain escarpment shuts in the Kisumu plain. From this vantage-point there is a range of view of a hundred miles.

On the march down to Kisumu, some fifteen miles, a visit was paid to Ogadas, on the crest of the escarpment. Back in Kisumu I found the streets crowded with representatives of tribes far and wide, from the man who fancies himself in a grotesque adaptation of European costume, to those more primitive members of society who have wandered in out of curiosity, clothed in the main in their village costume. They may be seen wrapt in thought and sunshine, with a minimum attempt to comply with the rules of society, as they have come to understand them.